صندوق باندورا

Pandora's Box

retold by Henriette Barkow

illustrated by Diana Mayo

Arabic translation by Dr. Sajida Fawzi

MANTRA
LINGUA

عاش منذ القِدَم عند بدء الخليقة آلِهة والاهات.

جلس زيوس ، ملك الآلهة ، على قمة جبل اولِمبس وتأمّل الأرض فوجدها جميلة ولكنّ شيئًا ما كان مفقوداً فيها. وأمعن النظر فيها ثمّ قرر أن ما تحتاجة الأرض هو الحيوانات والطيور والأسماك.

Long long ago, at the beginning of time, lived gods and goddesses.

Zeus, the king of the gods, sat on Mount Olympus and thought that the earth was beautiful but also that something was missing. He looked closer and decided what was needed on earth were animals and birds and fishes.

صندوق باندورا

أسطورة يونانية

لليونانيين القدماء مكانة أساسية في الحضارة الغربية. وفي مجتمعاتهم القديمة كانت الأساطير جزءٍ ألا يتجزأ من الفن والأدب والدين والتعليم. وفي الوقت الحاضر نستطيع أن نتفهّم بعض الشيىء طبيعة اليونانيين القدماء وتراثهم من خلال أساطيرهم.

The ancient Greeks stand at the cornerstone of Western civilisation. Their mythology was an integral part of the art, literature, religion and education of ancient Greek society. It is through their mythology that we today can gain some understanding of what the ancient Greeks were like as a people and a culture.

First published 2002 by Mantra Lingua
Global House, 303 Ballards Lane, London N12 8NP
www.mantralingua.com

Text copyright © 2002 Henriette Barkow
Illustration copyright © 2002 Diana Mayo
Dual Language text copyright © 2002 Mantra Lingua Ltd
Audio copyright © Mantra Lingua 2008
This sound enabled edition published 2012

استدعى زيوس اليه تايتِن بروميثيوس وتايتِن اييميثيوس وكلّفهما بمهمة خلق كل
المخلوقات لتعيش على الأرض. وقال لهما " هذا كيس عطايا فيه بعض الخصائص
التميزة وباء مكانكما تقديمها لمخلوقاتكما. "

Zeus called the two Titans, Prometheus and Epimetheus, to him and
gave them the task of creating all the creatures to live on the earth.
"Here is a bag with some special gifts that you can give to your
creations," he told them.

وكان بروميثيوس و ايبيميثيوس أخوين وكغيرهم من الإخوان كان لكل منهما ميزات قوية وأخرى ضعيفة. فقد كان بروميثيوس، اسمه يعني المتكهن، هو الأذكى إلى حد بعيد وكما يشير اسمه فهو عادة يستطيع التنبأ بالمستقبل. ولذا فانه حذّر ايبيميثيوس قائلاً "لن اكون دائماً هنا، فما عليك إلّا أن تحرص على ماقد يقدّمه زيوس من عطايا."

Prometheus and Epimetheus were brothers, and like many brothers each had his own strengths and weaknesses. Prometheus, whose name means forethought, was by far the cleverer, and as his name suggests, he could often see into the future. Thus it was that he warned Epimetheus: "I won't always be here, so take great care with any gift that Zeus may give."

رغم أن ايبيميثيوس لم يكن بذكاء أخيه الّا أنه كان 'يجيد عمل صناعة الأشياء بيديه مثل عمل النحّات والنجّار. فصنع كل المخلوقات التي يمكن ان يتذكرها وأعطى لكل منها ميزة مختلفة وجدها في كيس عطايا زيوس. فاعطى لبعض المخلوقات رقبة طويلة وأعطى البعض الآخر جلود مخططة وأذناب أو مناقير وريش.

Although Epimetheus wasn't as clever as his brother, he was good at making things, like a sculptor or a carpenter. He created all the creatures that he could think of and gave them different gifts from Zeus' bag. Some he gave long necks, others he gave stripes and tails, beaks and feathers.

وعندما انتهى من صنع كل المخلوقات طلب من بروميثيوس أن يراها

وسأله " مارأيك فيها؟ "

" انها فعلاً مخلوقات رائعة " أجاب بروميثيوس.

ونظر بروميثيوس الى الأرض وفكّر بنوع آخر من المخلوقات ـ مخلوقات تشبه

الآلهة في شكلها فأخذ شيئاً من الطين وأضاف اليه قليلاً من الماء وصنع منه

ألا نسان الأول. ثم صنع له بعض الأصدقاء كي لا يكون وحيداً.

When he had made all the creatures he showed them to Prometheus.
"What do you think?" he asked his brother.
"They are truly wonderful," said Prometheus.
Looking across the earth Prometheus then had the idea for another
kind of creature - one that would be modelled on the gods. He took
some clay and added some water and moulded the first man.
Then he made him some friends so that man wouldn't be lonely.

وعندما انتهى من العمل قدّم ما صنعه من مخلوقات الى زيوس الذي نفخ فيها الحياة.

When he had finished he showed his creations to Zeus who breathed life into them.

وقام كلّ من بروميثيوس و ابيميثيوس بتعليم الإنسان رعاية نفسه.

وبقيا على الأرض وسكنا مع الإنسان و علّماه الصيد وبناء الأكواخ والزراعة.

وفي ذات يوم ذهب بروميثيوس ليفتش في كيس زيوس عن عطية لمخلوقاته

ولكنه وجد الكيس خالياً. فقد أعطي الخرطوم للفيل والذيل الطويل للقرد

والزئير العظيم للأسد والطيران للطيور حتى نفذت الهدايا.

Prometheus and Epimetheus taught man how to look after himself. They
stayed on earth and lived with man teaching him how to hunt, build shelters and
grow food.

One day Prometheus went to Zeus' bag to find a gift for his creations but the
bag was empty. The trunk had been given to the elephant, the long tail had been
given to the monkey, the biggest roar to the lion, flight to the birds and so it
went until there were no more gifts.

واصبح بروميثيوس معجباً بمخلوقاته وأراد أن يقدّم للإنسان شيئاً متميزاً يجعل

حياته أسهل. وعندما كان يتأملّ مخلوقاته واذا به يفكر بذلك الشيىء المتميز ـ انه النار.

سيعطي النار للإنسان ولكن النار هي مِلْكُ الآلهة ولكي يعطيها للإنسان لم يكن

أمام بروميثيوس الّا طريقة واحدة وهي أن يقوم بسرقتها. وتحت غطاء الظلام تسلّق

بروميثيوس جبل اولِمبس وسرق شعلة صغيرة وأعطاها للإنسان وعلّمه كيف يبقيها

ملتهبة وعلّمه كل الذي يستطيع أن يفعله باستعمال النار.

Prometheus, who had grown very fond of his creations, wanted something special to give to man, something that would make his life easier. And as he watched his creation the idea came to him – fire. He would give man fire.

Now fire belonged to the gods and the only way that Prometheus could give fire to man was by stealing it.

Under the cloak of darkness Prometheus climbed Mount Olympus and stole a tiny flame and gave it to man. He taught him how to keep the flame alive and all that man could do with fire.

وسرعان ما لاحظ زيوس أن الانسان يملك شيئاً لا يعود له وانما يعود الى الآلهة و هبة الآلهة لا

ليمكن استر جاعها. وغضب زيوس غضباً شديداً وبكل ما كان عنده من ثورة الاهية و غضب

قرّر أن يقتصّ من كلّ من بروميثيوس والإنسان.

قبض زيوس على بروميثيوس وقيده بسلاسل على سفح جبل و كادت آلامه أن تكون غير محتملة

ولكن لم يكن ذلك كافياً لأن زيوس أراد أن يجعل بروميثيوس ليعاني أكثر من هذا.

It didn't take long for Zeus to see that man had something that didn't belong to him, something that belonged to the gods and a gift given by a god could not be taken back. Zeus was furious and with all the rage and wrath of a god he decided to punish both Prometheus and man.

Zeus grabbed Prometheus and chained him to a cliff. The pain was almost unbearable but that wasn't enough for Zeus, he wanted Prometheus to suffer even more.

فأرسل زيوس نسراً ليشقّ كبد بروميثيوس. وفي كلّ ليلة يلتئم كبده
ولكن يعود النسر اليه كل صباح ليعذبه أكثر وأكثر.

ولم يكن نهاية لهذا الألم لذا فان بروميثيوس تُرِك ليعاني ألى الأبد من دون أمل.

So Zeus sent an eagle to tear out Prometheus' liver. Every night his
liver would heal and every morning the eagle would return, to torment
and torture Prometheus even more.

This was pain without ending, and thus Prometheus was doomed to
suffer forever without hope.

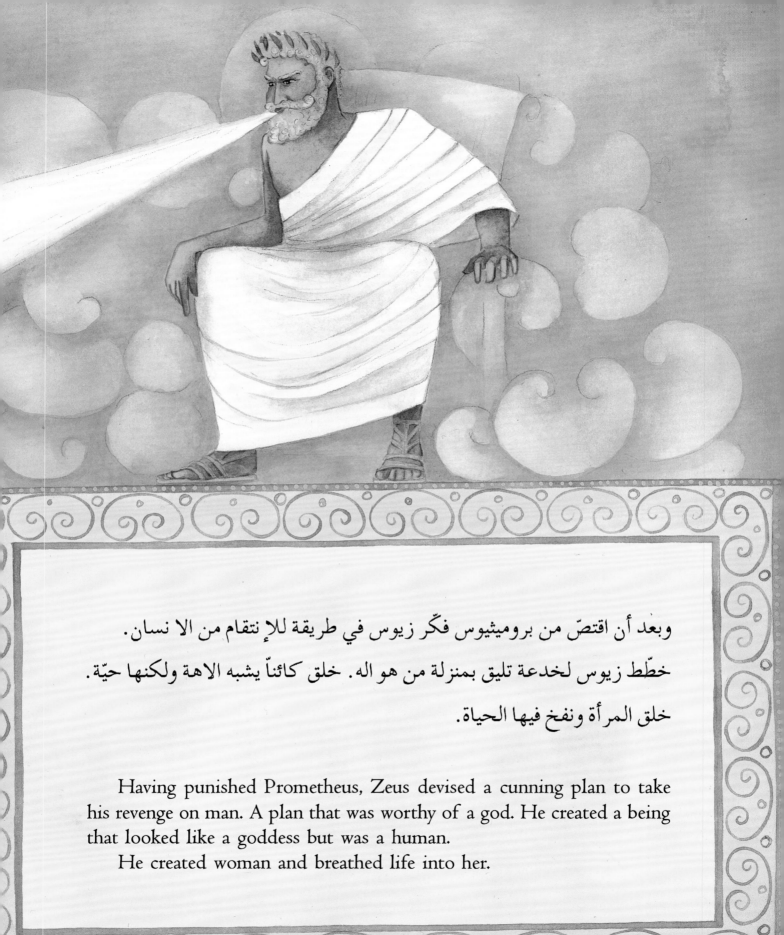

وبعد أن اقتصّ من بروميثيوس فكّر زيوس في طريقة للإنتقام من الإنسان.
خطّط زيوس لخدعة تليق بمنزلة من هو اله. خلق كائناً يشبه الاهة ولكنها حيّة.

خلق المرأة ونفخ فيها الحياة.

Having punished Prometheus, Zeus devised a cunning plan to take
his revenge on man. A plan that was worthy of a god. He created a being
that looked like a goddess but was a human.
He created woman and breathed life into her.

ودعا زيوس بقية الآلهة ذكوراً واناثاً الى جانبه وطلب من
كلّ منهم أن يقدّم هبة للمرأة. ومن ضمن هبات كثيرة فقد
وهبها أفروديت هبة الجمال وأثينا وهبها الحكمة ووهبها
هيرميس الكلام المعسول و أبولّو وهبها الحس الموسيقي.
وأطلق عليها زيوس اسم بندورا وأرسلها لتعيش على الأرض.

Zeus called the other gods and goddess to his side and asked
them each to give woman a gift. Among the many attributes,
Aphrodite gave woman beauty, Athena gave her wisdom, Hermes
gave her a clever tongue and Apollo gave her the gift of music.
Zeus named her Pandora and sent her to live on earth.

كان من الصعب مقاومتها فهي امرأة من خلْق السماء لها هبات

الآلهة فوقع ايبيميثيوس في حبّ باندورا.

وفي يوم زفافهما أعطاهما زيوس صندوق جميل أخّاذ وقال لهما

" استمتعا بجمال هذه الهدية واحرصا عليها جيداً. ولكن تذكرا

أن هذا الصندوق يجب الاّ يُفتح أبداً ."

A woman made in heaven, with the gifts of the gods, was impossible to resist
and Epimetheus fell in love with Pandora.

On their wedding day Zeus gave them a beautiful and intriguing box.
"Enjoy the beauty of this gift, and guard it well. But remember this
- this box must never be opened."

فيى البداية كان ايبيميوس و باندورا سعيدين جداً. كان العالم غنياً و مسالماً.
لم يكن هناك حروب أو أمراض ولا أحزان أو معاناة. وبينما كان ايبيميثيوس
خارج البيت طول اليوم فان باندورا استعملت هبتها في حب الإستطلاع بحكمة بالغة.
فابتدعت طرقاً جديدة فيى تحضير الطعام والعزف على الموسيقى ودرست الحيوانات
والحشرات من حولها. وساعدت باندورا الانسان على التعرف على طرق جديدة
لاستعمال النار فيى الطبخ وصهر العادن.

At first Pandora and Epimetheus were very happy. The world was a rich
and peaceful place. There were no wars or illnesses, no sadness or suffering.
  While Epimetheus was out all day Pandora used her gift of curiosity
wisely. She found new ways to prepare their food and new music to play.
She studied the animals and insects around her. Pandora showed man new
ways of using fire to cook and work metals.

ولكنْ حب الإستطلاع هو سيف ذو حدّين ومع كل الأشياء الحسنة التي قامت بها باندورا ولكنها لم تستطع أن تنسى الصندوق المغلق. فهي تذهب وتنظر اليه كل يوم وتتذكر كلمات زيوس "يجب ألاّ يُفتح هذا الصندوق."

But curiosity is a double-edged sword, and for all the good that Pandora had done she could not put the locked box out of her mind. Every day she would just go and have a look at it. And every day she remembered Zeus' words: "This box must never be opened!"

وبعد بضعة أشهر وجدت باندورا نفسها تجلس مرة أخرى أمام الصندوق.

وسألت نفسها "ما الضرر من أن ألقي نظرة في داخله؟"

"وما هو الشيء المرعب الذي يمكن أن يكون في داخله؟" ونظرت حولها

لتتأكد من أنها لوحدها وفتحت القفل بواسطة دّبوس كان في شعرها.

After some months had passed Pandora found herself sitting in front of the box again. "What harm would it do if I just sneaked a look inside?" she asked herself. "After all what could possibly be in there that is so terrible?" She looked around to make sure that she was alone and then she took a pin from her hair and carefully picked the lock.

وعندما انفتح القفل اندفع الغطاء بسرعة
وانفتح الصندوق. ومن الصعب جدا تفسيرالأشياء
المرعبة التي كانت مخزونة في ذلك الصندوق
والضرر الذي اندلع منه على العالم.

As soon as the lock opened, the lid flew back and the box burst open. It is hard to explain in words the terrible things that were stored within that box and the suffering that was unleashed upon the world.

وعندما رُفع الغطاء فاض من الصندوق الكره والطمع،
الطاعون والمرض وكل الأشياء المؤذية التي
نعاني منها اليوم.

When the lid was lifted, out flew hate and greed, pestilence and disease and all the terrible things that still torment us today.

وصدمت باندورا عندما رأت مافعلته ، فسحبت الغطاء وحاولت بكل قوتها غلق الصندوق .

وجلست متعبة على الأرض تبكي .

واذا بصوت رقيق يناديها "دعيني أخرج ! دعيني أخرج !"

ونظرت باندورا الى أعلى لِترى من أين يأتي هذا الصوت الرقيق .

Pandora was so shocked when she saw what she had done, that she
grabbed the lid and forced it down again with all her strength.
Exhausted she sat on the ground and sobbed.
"Let me out! Let me out!" cried a small and gentle voice.
Pandora looked up to see where this sweet voice was coming from.

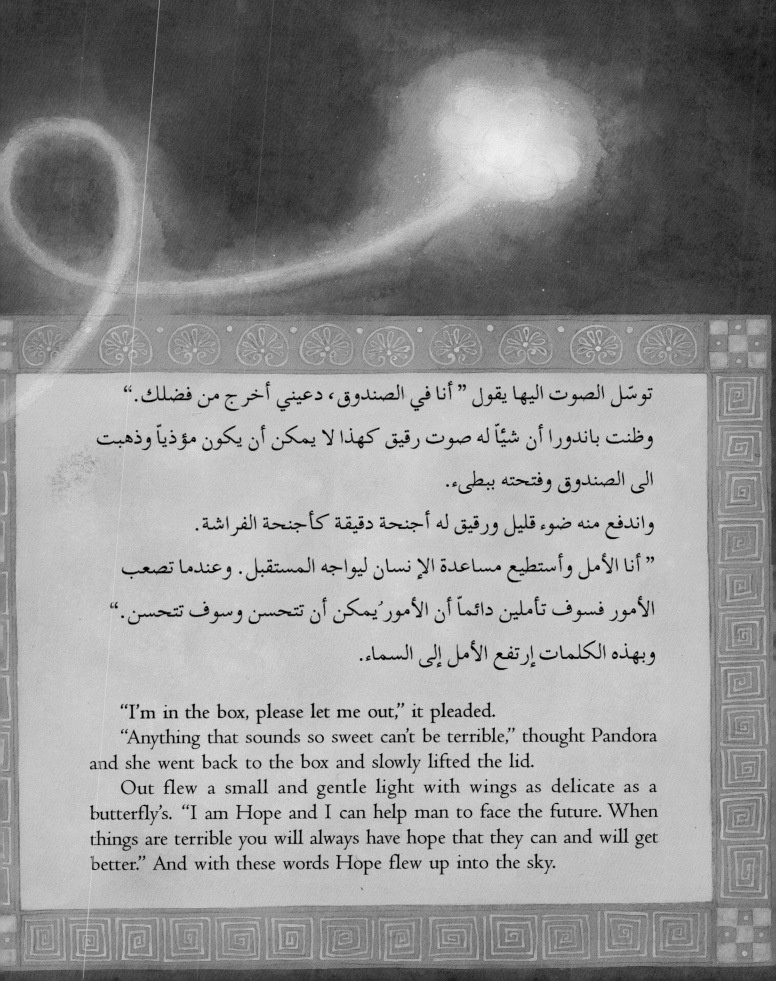

توسّل الصوت اليها يقول " أنا في الصندوق، دعيني أخرج من فضلك."

وظنت باندورا أن شيئاً له صوت رقيق كهذا لا يمكن أن يكون مؤذياً وذهبت الى الصندوق وفتحته ببطىء.

واندفع منه ضوء قليل ورقيق له أجنحة دقيقة كأجنحة الفراشة.

" أنا الأمل وأستطيع مساعدة الإنسان ليواجه المستقبل. وعندما تصعب الأمور فسوف تأملين دائماً أن الأمور يمكن أن تتحسن وسوف تتحسن."

وبهذه الكلمات إرتفع الأمل إلى السماء.

"I'm in the box, please let me out," it pleaded.

"Anything that sounds so sweet can't be terrible," thought Pandora and she went back to the box and slowly lifted the lid.

Out flew a small and gentle light with wings as delicate as a butterfly's. "I am Hope and I can help man to face the future. When things are terrible you will always have hope that they can and will get better." And with these words Hope flew up into the sky.

وفي طريقه عِبْرَ الأرض مرَّ الأمل على بروميثيوس وهو مقيد الى الجبل بسلاسل ولمس قلبه.

وقد يحتاج الى بِضْعٍ من آلاف سنين أخرى قبل أن يطلق سراحه هيراكليس ولكن هذه ، وكما يُقال ، هي قصة أخرى.

As Hope journeyed across the earth it passed Prometheus chained to the mountain and touched his heart.

It would take a few more thousand years before Heracles set him free but that, as they say, is another story.